The First Americans

116248

The First Americans

Pamela Odijk

M

The First Americans

Contents

The First Americans: timeline

First migrants crossed from Asia to North
America, via the Bering landbridge, a landbridge
that connected Siberia and Alaska during the last
Ice-Age. When the earth's climate became
warmer, this landbridge went underwater and the
Bering Strait was formed.

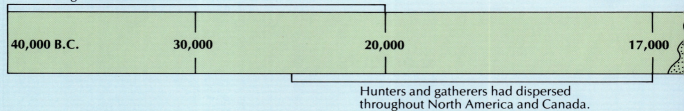

| 40,000 B.C. | 30,000 | 20,000 | 17,000 |

Hunters and gatherers had dispersed
throughout North America and Canada.

Eskimo people begin
to use the sea
as a source of food.

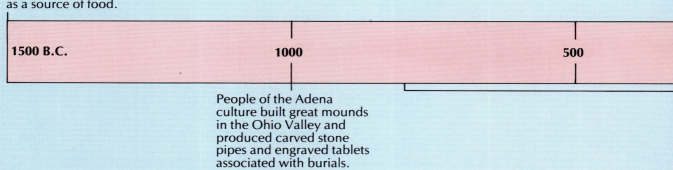

| 1500 B.C. | 1000 | 500 |

People of the Adena
culture built great mounds
in the Ohio Valley and
produced carved stone
pipes and engraved tablets
associated with burials.

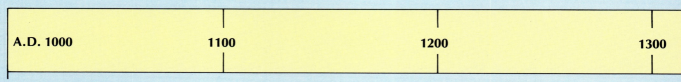

| A.D. 1000 | 1100 | 1200 | 1300 |

Viking sea-farers
reached Newfoundland.

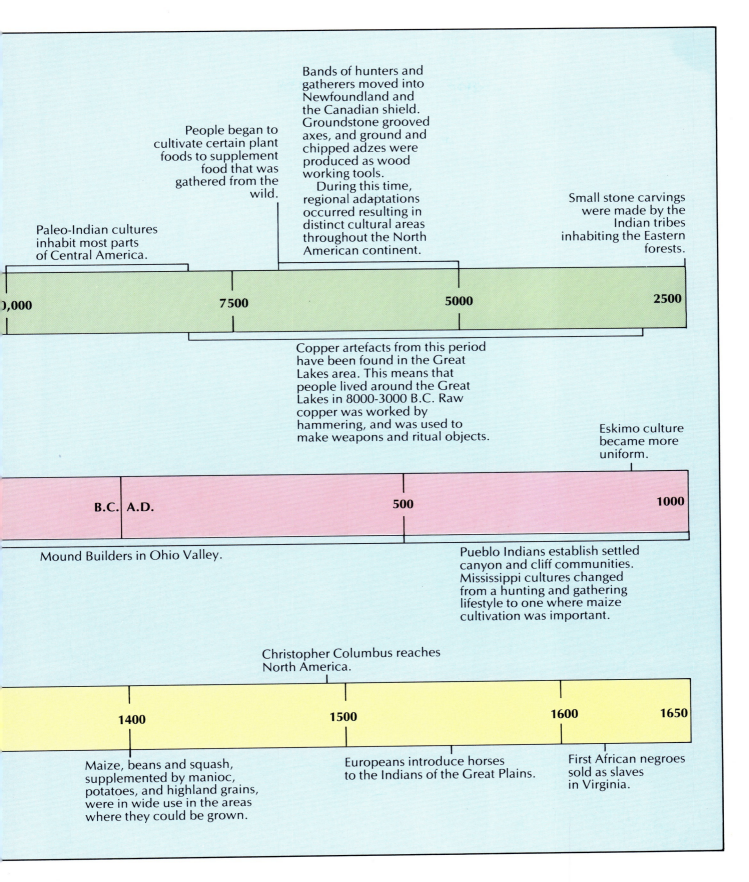

Bands of hunters and gatherers moved into Newfoundland and the Canadian shield. Groundstone grooved axes, and ground and chipped adzes were produced as wood working tools.
During this time, regional adaptations occurred resulting in distinct cultural areas throughout the North American continent.

People began to cultivate certain plant foods to supplement food that was gathered from the wild.

Small stone carvings were made by the Indian tribes inhabiting the Eastern forests.

Paleo-Indian cultures inhabit most parts of Central America.

0,000   7500   5000   2500

Copper artefacts from this period have been found in the Great Lakes area. This means that people lived around the Great Lakes in 8000-3000 B.C. Raw copper was worked by hammering, and was used to make weapons and ritual objects.

Eskimo culture became more uniform.

B.C. A.D.   500   1000

Mound Builders in Ohio Valley.

Pueblo Indians establish settled canyon and cliff communities. Mississippi cultures changed from a hunting and gathering lifestyle to one where maize cultivation was important.

Christopher Columbus reaches North America.

1400   1500   1600   1650

Maize, beans and squash, supplemented by manioc, potatoes, and highland grains, were in wide use in the areas where they could be grown.

Europeans introduce horses to the Indians of the Great Plains.

First African negroes sold as slaves in Virginia.

Map Legend

- Eastern Forests
- South-West Desert
- California
- North-West Plateau
- Great Basin
- Arctic
- Sub-Arctic
- Meso-America
- Great Plains/Prairie Lands

Map Labels

Arctic Ocean

0   1000   2000
kms

Bering Sea

Bering Strait

Aleutian Islands

Alaska Range

Alaska Peninsula

Gulf of Alaska

Mackenzie Range

Baffin Bay

Baffin Island

Great Bear Lake

Great Slave Lake

Hudson Bay

Labrador Sea

Rocky Mountains

Coast Ranges

Newfoundland

Saint Lawrence River

Lake Superior

Lake Huron

Lake Ontario

Lake Michigan

Great Nevada Basin

Great Salt Lake

Missouri River

Colorado River

Ozark Plateau

Ohio River

Appalachian Mountains

Atlantic Ocean

Mississippi River

Sierra Madre Occidental

Rio Grande

Sierra Madre Oriental

WEST INDIES

Pacific Ocean

Baja California

Gulf of Mexico

Caribbean Sea

North America

During the last Ice Age, Siberia and Alaska were joined by the Bering landbridge.

N

The First Americans: Introduction

The Europeans who followed Columbus to the **New World** (the Americas) found the large continent inhabited by people of many different cultures, whose ancestors had arrived there by way of north-east Asia and Alaska. They came originally from the **Old World**, that is, that part of the world that was known before the discovery of the Americas comprising Europe, Asia and Africa. Some scholars believe these people, who were hunters and gatherers, crossed into Alaska as early as 20,000 years ago in search of the animals they hunted, across a **landbridge** where Bering Strait is now located.

Our knowledge of the peoples who inhabited the North American continent before written records were kept comes mainly from the work of **archaeologists** and **anthropologists**. The oldest culture found by archaeologists, to date, is called the **Paleo-Indian** culture. These people were a Stone Age culture, who were hunters and foragers. They lived a nomadic existence moving around in bands of 30 to 40 people or as family units. Their tools included spears and darts with double-edged stone blades, and stone knives, scrappers, drills and hammer-stones. Their stone implements provided a strong edge for shaping other materials, and for preparing gathered plants and killed animals. Archaeologists have been able to establish that Paleo-Indian cultures were dispersed throughout most of central North America 10,000 to 12,000 years ago.

Around this time, the last Ice Age came to an end, and changes in the climate brought changes to the animal and plant life. The Paleo-Indian cultures gradually spread out. The next 7,000 years was a period of regional adaptation by the Indian ancestors to the diverse north American environment.

During this long period, each group learned to adapt to their particular environment and in so doing, each group developed its own distinctive culture.

The North American continent can be divided into a number of major cultural areas:

Mt McKinley, Alaska. The Indian ancestors migrated to a landscape of vast ice sheets and mountain ranges when they crossed the Bering landbridge.

Eastern Forests remains of some of the oldest cultures such as Ohio and Adena Mound builders
Great Plains
South-West Desert remains of Folsom Culture (Paleo-India) found in this area
California
North-West Coast and Plateau
Great Basin
Arctic Inuit
Sub-Arctic

Much of the magnificence of these first Americans was destroyed as the Europeans took over their land from the 16th century onward. Although Indian scientific knowledge and cultural achievements were many and well-advanced, they could not withstand the impact of the European invasion.

In 1492 Christopher Columbus made landfall at an island in the Bahamas, which he named San Salvador. He thought he had reached Asia, and the people he saw were the Indians of India. He had instead discovered the home of the first Americans. The Indian population at that time has been estimated as being in between one to two million, north of the present Mexican border, and eleven million south of there.*

In the years that followed Columbus's arrival in North America, the Europeans made their way to this continent and invaded and exploited the land, and dispossesed the people who inhabited it.

* This book is about the first Americans who inhabited the North American continent, as the cultures of the Maya, Incas and Aztecs have been dealt with comprehensively in other books of this series.

The Indian tribes of the North-West coast of America carved huge totem poles from tree trunks. This totem pole, known as the ''Hole-In-the-Sky'' pole, was originally used as a ceremonial entrance to a particular clan's house. Each clan possessed its own history and traditions in the form of myths and legends. The images on this pole reflect the clan's history, and are a combination of crest and ancestor figures.

The Importance of Landforms and Climate

The North American continent is shaped like an inverted triangle and covers 24,230,000 square kilometres (9,355,000 square miles), which reaches from the **Arctic** north to the subtropical south. It encompasses landscapes as diverse as snow peaked mountains and desert sands. Huge mountain ranges and huge rivers form the character of the northern American landscape. The ice caps which covered the American continent 10,000 to 25,000 years ago formed many of the geographical features, including the shape of the land, the size, shape and drainage of the Great Lakes, the path of the Hudson River, and the shape and size of the Great Central Basin.

Right: autumn colours of the North-Eastern forests, which are made up of maple, oak, birch and beech trees.

Below: map of the North American continent showing the main landforms.

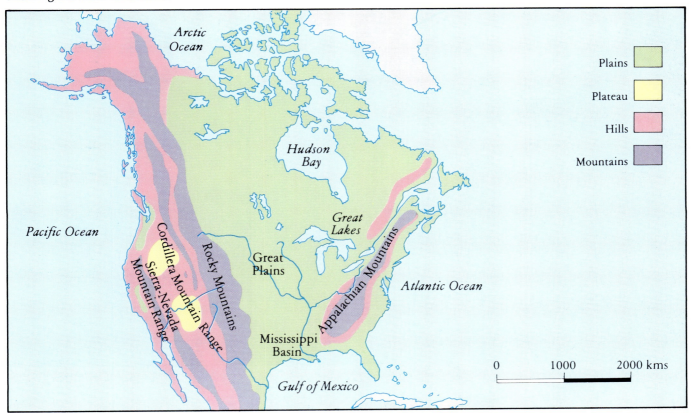

Plains

Plateau

Hills

Mountains

Climate

The climatic conditions encountered by the Paleo-Indian groups 17,000 years ago were much different to the climate found in the United States today. Ice sheets dominated the northern part of the continent, and the southerly mountain ranges. The presence of these ice sheets produced a colder and wetter climate.

About 10,000 years ago, the last Ice Age came to an end as the earth's climate became warmer, and by about 3,000 years ago it started to resemble current climatic conditions.

Although much of North America lies in a temperate climatic zone there are areas which lie in the cold arctic north and in the tropical south. Onshore winds bring rain to the western part of the continent and these are blocked by the Cascade Mountains and the Sierra Nevada Mountains so the small narrow lowland receives heavy rainfall. Further inland from the Pacific the land becomes drier and lies in the rainshadow of the mountains. Great areas of desert occur west of the Rocky Mountains extending from Alaska to Mexico.

Temperatures vary throughout the North American continent. Along the west coast there is very little difference in temperature between summer and winter because of the influence of the sea, while in the north and central part of the country there are great extremes with temperatures varying from $-40°C$ ($-104°F$) at its coldest to $45°C$ ($113°F$) at its hottest. Hours of daylight also vary. In the northern areas such as Alaska there is almost continuous daylight during summer.

Massive buttes and mesas in Monument Valley, Navaho Desert. The Indian groups of the South-West Desert inhabited this landscape.

Natural Plants, Animals and Birds

The North American continent supports a diversity of plant and animal life. By the time the Europeans arrived thick forests covered almost half of the land and stretched west for over 1,600 kilometres (993 miles) where they gave way to tall grasses of the **prairies**. These grasses often grew to heights of 2 metres (7 feet). Further west forests also covered the slopes of the mountains while high valleys in the Rocky Mountains were covered with short grasses. On the high tablelands and lowlands, dry bushes grew along with tough spiny grasses. In the desert areas tough spiny grasses grew along with thorn bushes. Some areas were so dry and had such poor soils that nothing grew at all. After the Europeans arrived, much of the land was cleared for settlements.

Animals

The animal life the American Indian ancestors encountered during the last Ice Age 20,000 to 10,000 years ago included long-horned bison, giant ground sloths, large carnivorous wolves and hairy mammoths.

As the last Ice Age came to an end, the changing climatic conditions, such as warmer temperatures and lower rainfall, caused the vegetation to alter. In the Great Plains, this caused problems of adjustment for the mammoths. They became extinct about 10,000 years ago, and the buffalo came to be the dominant herd of the Plains.

The animal and plant life adapted to the changing environment. The Indians relied on a variety of wild plants and animals as a source of food. Wild plant foods gathered included nuts, grass and plant seeds, roots and bulbs, fruits and berries, and wild rice.

Remains of huge piles of shells found by archaeologists along river banks and seacoasts indicate the variety of sea life used as food by the American Indians.

The grizzly bear inhabits the tundra and forested regions of the North American continent.

The large animals that roamed the land and were hunted included bison (buffaloes), caribou, pronghorn antelopes, mountain sheep and goats, black and brown bears, badgers, raccoons, opossums and wolverines. Many of these animals became extinct, as they were exploited from the 16th century onward by the European and white American fur trade. In the freshwater streams and water catchments, salmon, trout and striped bass provided abundant food for the tribes along the northern coasts.

About 9,000 years ago, the American Indians began the domestication of plants, that is, they began to cultivate crops for their own consumption. By 1492, hundreds of species of plants had been domesticated, not only for food, but for raw materials such as cotton, poisons and stimulants.

Crops, Herds and Hunting

The majority of cultures inhabiting the North American continent before European contact were **nomadic**. Each nomadic group consisted of about 20 to 50 people, who supported themselves by collecting wild plant and animal food. They moved about following the seasonal food supply. About 9,000 years ago, some groups began to grow their own plant foods, to supplement their diet of foraged foods.

By the 15th century A.D., maize, beans, squash, **manioc**, potatoes and grains were in wide use where they could be grown. Most cultivation was slash and burn. The vegetation had to be cleared and burnt before seeds could be planted with a digging stick or hoe, the two main farming tools. The plough was unknown until introduced by Europeans.

As certain groups began to cultivate crops, permanent houses and villages became established. In the Eastern Forests area, the Indian societies cultivated seed plants, gourds and squash. Maize cultivation developed after A.D. 700, and in the 10th century beans became an important crop.

Many villages and towns developed on the flood plains of central and lower Mississippi River, in about 1000 B.C. Most of these towns had palisades and flat-topped rectangular mounds that were used as bases for temples.

In the South-West Desert area, crop cultivation began in about 5000 B.C. These groups built permanent dwellings in the cliff faces. The Spanish called these people the "Pueblos" people. (Pueblos is a Spanish word that means town).

These groups established villages consisting of about 100 people belonging to a common family group.

The Pueblos Indians built permanent dwellings in cliff faces, as shown by these cliff ruins at Mesa Verde, Colorado.

Subterranean winter houses built by the Inuit were dug about 1 metre (3–4 feet) into the ground, lined with timber and covered in sod.

Folsom Culture

One of the oldest Paleo-Indian cultures identified so far by archaeologists is the Folsom culture. Artefacts from this culture have been found at Folsom, Arizona, in the South-West Desert area. This culture was characterised by their fluted, double-edged knives and spears. Implements found that are dated as 11,000–10,000 years old include scrapers, chisels, knives, bone awls and needles. These implements have been found at sites where remains of the extinct long-horned bison were found, which indicates that these people hunted the prehistoric bison. But it is unlikely that they were entirely dependent on the bison as a food source. Archaeological evidence suggests that small game were also hunted, and seeds, berries and wild vegetable foods were gathered. Because this was a nomadic hunting and gathering culture, shelters would have been temporary or semi-permanent.

The Arctic

The Inuit (Eskimo) culture is at least 4,000 years old. They hunted sea-mammals and fish. They lived in small isolated villages, sometimes consisting of one family only. The family unit was important. Inuit settlements were semi-permanent, in that they relied on migratory animals and fish, and had to move seasonally to the food source. Though hunting conditions were harsh, the animals and fish, once caught, provided raw materials for fuel, shelter, clothing, food, utensils and weapons.

The most common houses were semi-subterranean sod houses. Tents were used in less harsh conditions as semi-permanent shelter, and in very harsh Arctic areas, people protected themselves within dome shaped snow houses called **igloos**.

Sub-Arctic

The Sub-Arctic groups lived in an area with harsh conditions, which were mainly cold and wet, with heavy rains and deep snow. Caribou and moose were the main source of food for these hunters. Fish were also caught. Wild plant foods that were foraged included berries, roots and seeds.

As these people were mainly nomadic, most forms of shelter were semi-permanent and included brushwood shelters, tipis and tents. In harsher conditions, subterranean pit shelters were common.

North-West Coast

The rivers and streams of the North-West Coast provided an abundant supply of shellfish and fish, especially salmon, as a food source.

Candlefish were used for oil. Small sea mammals were hunted, and plants and berries were collected. Land animals such as goats and sheep were also hunted.

North-West Plateau

The people who inhabited this area were hunters and foragers who established permanent villages. They lived in an area that had an abundance of animals, plants and fish, especially salmon, which ensured a continual source of food.

Interior of a house, North-West coast. The floor space was built about 1 metre (3–4 feet) into the ground. The carved house post (left rear) supported the ridge beams.

The Sioux of the Great Plains dwelt in tipis.

Great Plains

The people who followed, hunted and lived on buffalo, learned to hunt with great skill. They respected the buffaloes important place in nature, and never killed more than they needed. The buffalo herd not only ensured a source of food, but also provided hides for clothes and shelters (**tipis**), thread for sewing, oil for cooking, and often the rough underside of the tongue was used as a brush. Other small animals such as elk, antelope, and bear were also hunted. Berries and other wild plant foods were collected, and some cereal crops were obtained by trade.

As the tribes who inhabited the Plains followed the buffalo herds, housing was semi-permanent. The most common Plains dwelling was the **tipi**, although brushwood shelters and tents were also used.

Eastern Forests

These people were settled farmers who grew corn, beans, pumpkins and tobacco. Wild deer were hunted, and wild plants, fish and shellfish were collected.

Many cultures flourished in this area. Among some groups, such as the Iroquois, women played a prominent role in village leadership. Men cleared the fields, and women did the farming.

One of the oldest Eastern Forest cultures so far recognised by archaeologists is the Mound Builders who appeared in about 1000 B.C. They are called "mound builders" because they built huge earthworks, or mounds which they used as burial sites.

California

The groups that lived in the California area were mainly foragers. Oak trees grew in abundance, so acorns were collected and processed as a main food. The Californians also relied heavily on grass seeds, and other wild plant foods. Along the coast, shellfish and fish were collected and, toward the interior, game such as bears, rabbits and deer were hunted.

Groups of about 100 people bonded by a common dialect moved about as small villages. Houses included temporary brushwood shelters, or semi-permanent tipis.

South-West Desert Area

These were farming communities, who established villages and towns. Maize was the staple food although beans, squash and sunflowers were also grown. From A.D. 400—1300, the ancestors of the Pueblos people, the Anasazi, practised agriculture. They built multi-storey dwellings made from mud, stone and beams in the cliff sides.

Kinship, Marriage and Inheritance

Most Indian American societies were organised on the basis of kinship. Clans existed in many cultural areas, and these clans dictated strict taboos in relation to marriage. Marriage between close relatives, and in some societies, any relative, was strictly forbidden. Women were married usually at the age of 12, to older men (18—19 years old). In most societies, men were encouraged to have two or more wives. If a woman's husband died, she would be encouraged to marry her late husband's brother, or her sister's husband.

Residence after marriage was usually with the husband's family, but residence with the wife's family was common in the Eastern Forests and South-West Deserts.

Inheritance usually followed the post-marital residence pattern.

This jug, decorated with spiral design, was made by the Anasazi of the South-West desert.

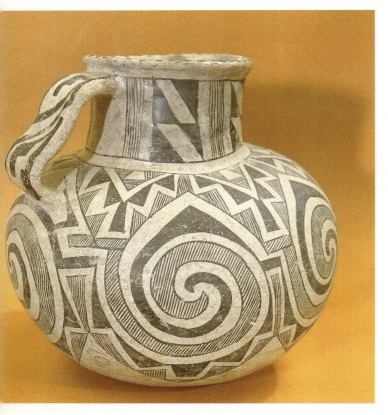

Work

The work of men and women was concerned with everyday existence and survival. Men and women shared the work depending on local customs and traditions. For example, in some parts of the continent men were potters, weavers and sewers of hides, while in other places this was the work of women. Water pails, carrying containers, implements for winnowing wild rice, and troughs were made, often from bark in areas where trees were plentiful. Wooden containers were more common in the North-West. Baskets were made by people of the plateau areas for gathering plant food and for storage. Some woven containers were sealed with pitch to make them waterproof and they were used as buckets or for cooking. In areas where clays were available, pottery vessels were made for household use.

The weaving of mats, bags and cloth was also a part of everyday work. This work was usually regarded as women's work.

The dressing of animal skins was important work as hides were used to make many items such as house walls, utensils and clothing.

Slaves

Slavery was practised in many Indian societies. Slaves were usually prisoners obtained in raids or wars, and were at the mercy of their owners. They could be killed or sacrificed by their owners, either upon the owner's death, or for religious purposes and frequently at a **potlatch**. Slaves were treated as the lowest order in most societies, compelled to do menial work and usually forced to eat inferior food.

Food and Medicine

Most American Indian cultures traditionally relied upon the harvest of wild plant foods, supplemented with animal foods. The most important foods included nuts, grass and seeds, roots and bulbs, fruit and berries, and wild rice, fish and shellfish, and both small and large game.

Many plant foods gathered by the Indians contained poisons which had to be removed before the food could be eaten. In California, acorns were an important food. The acorns contained tannin which was removed by **leaching** with water.

Grinding

Many foods needed to be shelled, hulled and ground before they could be used. **Pestles and mortars** and grinding stones were used for this. Flour made from grinding grains was used to make a **gruel** such as **hominy**, and breads such as **piki bread**. Grain was also made into porridge or meal.

Cooking Methods

The Indian cultures used thousands of different recipes, none of which were written down. Most people preferred to cook their food with the exception of the Inuit (Eskimos) who ate much of their food raw. Most food, especially vegetable and meat stews were boiled over or near a fire or by placing heated stones in a vessel with the food. The later method was used in areas where wood, bark, basketry and hide vessels were used. As pottery became more common this method was used less.

Earth ovens were also used. These were holes dug in the ground into which hot stones and food were placed, covered with leaves, bark and earth and left for many hours or overnight. This method of cooking could only be used in areas were the ground was unfrozen.

Preserving Methods

The food supply changed with the seasons so when food was plentiful (in summer) attempts were made to preserve and store it for the times of scarcity (winter). Whenever there was a surplus, such as after a hunting or fishing expedition, it was usually preserved by smoking or drying, either over a fire or in the sun. Using a fire was preferred as this kept flies and other pests away from the food. In very hot windy areas, sun drying was always used. The freezing of foods was practised in the Arctic and Sub-Arctic regions.

Parfleche bag made from rawhide by the Sioux of the Plains. Such bags were used to store pemmican.

Dried meat was pounded with stones to make a durable food called **pemmican**, which could be kept for years if necessary. Pemmican was made by softening the meat over a fire then pulverising it with fat, marrow, berries and fruit. This was packed in a **rawhide** container called a **parfleche**.

Medicine

American Indian medicine was closely related to religion. All Indians were religious and believed in "medicine", the spirit that protected them in everyday life and battle. This spirit was called upon through ceremonies and visions which involved prayers and incantations. Most native Americans believed that animals and natural objects possessed this spirit, and if violated would cause ill-health. Medicine was usually in the hands of the **shamans** whom the Europeans called medicine-men, although in some societies women were also shamans.

The authority of the shamans depended on their individual ability to bring about results. If a shaman lost several patients he was suspected of having lost his divine powers and the penalty for this was death.

Shamanistic practices differed. Among the Nootka (North-West Coast) there were two kinds of shamans: the *Uctak-u* who cured a person when sickness befell, and the *K.ok.oā'tsmaah* or soul workers whose special duty was to restore a person's wandering soul to its body.

The Songish people (who lived near present day Vancouver) also had two kinds of shamans: *squnä'am* who acquired his power through supernatural beings, and the *sīoua*, usually a woman who learned her skills from another *sī'oua*. The shamans of the Kutenai (North-West Plateau) had special lodges in which they prayed or contacted the spirits. The Hupa of California recognised two kinds of shamans: the dancing shamans who determined the cause of disease and decided upon the steps necessary for recovery, and the other shaman who "removed" the trouble by sucking it from the person's body. In Maidu country the shaman's children were obliged to become shamans or they would be killed by the spirits.

Procedures of the Shamans

First, an inquiry into the patient's symptons, dreams, and the breaking of any taboos. An examination of the patient's body to locate a source of pain occurred at this point.

This would be followed by a pronouncement of what the shaman considered to be, in his or her opinion, the cause of the condition and decided whether or not a cure was possible.

The shaman would then pray, sing, use ceremonial objects (such as rattles) and make passes over the affected part of the body with the hand.

A shaman would then often place his or her mouth over the most painful spot to extract the "cause" of the illness. Usually an object would be displayed in which the cause was believed to be contained. This could be a stone, hair or thorn produced by sleight-of-hand tricks. This object was then thrown away or destroyed.

Finally a "mysterious" powder or medicine would be administered, according to the shaman's decision as to the requirements of the case. Sometimes herbal remedies were used and other times mixtures which had no real curative powers except to convince the patient that by drinking or taking a substance they would recover. Shamans wished to exert as much mental influence as possible over the patient.

Shamans were known by different names in different societies.

Dakota	*wakan witshasha*: "mystery man"
	pejihuta witshasha: "grassroot man"
Navaho	*khathali*: "singer" or "chanter"
	izëëlini: "maker of medicines"
Apache (Plains)	*taivin*: "wonderful"
	izé: "medicine"

Clothes

Because the North American continent extended from the cold Arctic in the north to the tropical south, the people who inhabited the continent wore a variety of different clothes depending on the area in which they lived.

Body painting and tattooing, as well as head and tooth deformation were practised by most American Indian tribes. These forms of body adornation were believed to enhance beauty and indicate status. Other body adornments traditionally worn by most groups included: lip, ear and nose plugs, armbands, necklaces and headdresses.

The eagle feather war bonnet, worn by Sioux warriors, was a symbol of an outstanding warrior.

Above: pair of fringed leggings made from rawhide and beads by the Crow Indians of the Plains.

People of the Arctic

Inuit (Eskimos) used caribou hide as the main material for making clothes. **Parkas** were worn by men and women although women's parkas were larger so a child could be carried inside.

People of the North-West

In this area it was warm enough for men to go about naked in summer but usually they wore tunics of woven plant fibre. In colder months cloaks of animal skins were worn. The most highly prized fur was that of the sea otter.

These people were fond of ornaments and wore bracelets, belts, necklaces and leg bands of shells, teeth and claws of animals. Earrings were worn in pierced ears by men and women. Tattoos were also common and body paint (red, black and white) was worn on ceremonial occasions. **Head-binding** was practised to alter the shape of the forehead. A flattened forehead was considered a sign of beauty by the North-West cultures. Babies were bound in a wooden head press which caused the desired head deformation.

People of the Northern Plains

Here, men wore **breechcloths** and **moccasins**. Buffalo robes were worn during colder weather. Women wore calf-length dresses made of deer or elk hides sewn together and fringed at the bottom.

Both men and women wore mocassins and fur cloaks in winter, and plaited their hair into two plaits. Men wore feathers in their hair and feather headdresses. Ornaments included shells, beads, animal claws and teeth.

People of the South-East

Here men wore a buckskin breechcloth held in place by a belt at the waist. In colder weather cloaks of animal skins, woven bark or feathers were worn. Full leggings and moccasins were worn while travelling.

Women wore a wrap around skirt of buckskin, woven bark or bison hair which reached to the knees. No upper garment was worn in summer but cloaks were worn in winter by men and women. Knee length leggings were worn by women and occasionally moccasins.

Below: quilted moccasins made by the Sioux in 1885.

Religion and Rituals

Although there were many differences between the American Indian cultures of North America, they did have some important beliefs in common. All Indians felt very close to nature. All creatures were brothers, even those they hunted. The American Indians had a deep respect and love for the land, and believed that it belonged to all people, animals and plants.

The American Indians believed in a large variety of gods, ghosts and demons, as well as spirit helpers and personal guardian spirits who made contact through dreams and visions. Most cultures believed that if supernatural powers were offended some form of punishment would follow, such as illness or misfortune.

Shamans and priests played a large part in religious and social life. Shamans were believed to have the ability to make direct contact with the spirit world, and to seek and receive aid from a supernatural helper or to be possessed by spirits themselves. They acted on behalf of individuals or a group, depending on the culture of the people. Shamans and priests had different roles in different societies ranging from soothsayers and prophets, to trained priests.

The shamans' power, held in awe by others in a society, was often based on knowledge unavailable to others, such as being able to read the signs of nature and accurately predict rain or even eclipses. As well as using "magic" rituals, they also used substances known to have certain effects such as **curare**, a drug known to have anaesthetic qualities. This made their performance (and power) more convincing.

Although some groups observed no formal religious practices, most did and these often were accompanied by dancing, drumming and singing. Beliefs varied greatly from one group to another, and examples from some groups help to show this diversity.

Some Beliefs of the Sanpoil

The Sanpoil lived in the Plateau (Washington State) area and their religion emphasised vision quests. There were six kinds of spiritual personalities:

Sweat Lodge	The creator of animals, spirits and possibly humans.
The soul	Who lived near the heart in the human body. When the soul left the body, death was the result.
Ghosts	Of various kinds.
Spirits	Who had never resided in the human body. These took many forms, usually animal.
Spirit-ghosts	Which were transformed spirits resulting from the combination of a person's ghosts with his or her spirit helper.
Dangerous supernatural beings	Monsters, demons and ogres.

When a person died they went either to the end of the Milky Way in the sky or were transformed into a ghost and remained on earth.

Everyone sought at least one spirit helper and people were instructed in the art of acquiring a vision. After suitable training, the person would be sent in solitude to a designated place to await a vision of their spirit helper. An item to be left at the spot was given to the person to ensure that they reached their correct destination. Fasting and increasing discomfort such as exposure to cold induced hallucinations which were then accepted as visions of spirit helpers.

Some Navaho Beliefs

The Navaho (South-West Desert) believed in two types of people.

Earth People	Human beings and their ghosts after death.
Holy People	Other gods and spirits who travelled around on rainbows, sunbeams and flashes of lightning. These people lived in the underworld with the ghosts of the dead.

The most important of these two groups were:

Changing Woman	The creator and teacher of people and the main person of the Holy People.
Sun	Second in importance.
Hero Twins	Who were present at most ceremonies.

Below these were several other groups:
Failed-To-Speak People   such as Water Sprinkler, Fringed Mouth and Hunchback.
Animals and **personifications of natural forces**,   such as Coyote, Big Snake Man, Crooked Snake People, Thunder People and Wind People. The Navaho hunters of the south-eastern desert believed in nature spirits called **kachinas**.

The Navaho religion included sorcery and witchcraft. Navaho ceremonies, some of which could last all night, included: the Wind Chant, the Male Shooting Chant, the Big Star Chant, the Bead Chant, and the War Ceremony, all of which were re-enactments of their own myths.

The ceremonies included making prayer sticks which were placed at designated points and prayed over, and huge intricate sand paintings which sometimes needed forty people to work on them.

Some Beliefs of the North-West Coast Indians

There was no organised system of beliefs among any of the groups who inhabited the North-West Coast. Instead there were several un-related concepts which allowed for widely differing practices. Some of these included:

The belief that salmon were supernatural beings who voluntarily become fish. These beings were willing to sacrifice themselves for the benefit of people. If a fish was taken, its spirit was returned to the sea to be reincarnated if the bones of the fish were returned to the water after the flesh was eaten.

If the salmon-beings were offended, the fish would never return to the river.

Various rituals concerning the catching of the first salmon of the season took place. These included sprinkling the first fish with eagle down and red ochre, making speeches to the fish.

The belief that personal power could be gained by seeking contact with a spirit through prayer or a vision, and that all success was bestowed by spirits. From his or her personal spirit helper or other spirits, each person acquired songs, dances or knowledge as to how to make certain personal spiritual items or regalia.

Dances learnt in this way were called spirit dances and were performed at ceremonies during the winter months.

A belief in **totems**. These people carved huge statues from large trees. These statues were called **totem poles**. The carved images represented the ancestor spirits, gods and legends of the North-West Coast people.

This intricately carved stone pipe (A.D. 1200–1300) is believed to represent a warrior beheading a victim at a ritual sacrifice. The pipe is one of the ceremonial artefacts found at Spiro Mound in Oklahoma. Such pipes were for ceremonial smoking only.

Other Rituals of the Indians

Birth

Pregnant women observed special rituals from the time they realised they were carrying a baby, to the birth. Rituals and taboos often took the form of eating special foods, carrying out special behaviours and in some cases the mother was isolated from the rest of the society in a special hut or a screened off section of the dwelling until the birth of the child. Rituals became more frequent as the time of the birth drew near.

The birth usually took place in a special hut and the mother was helped by relatives or special midwives. Following the birth more food taboos and special behaviours were followed.

Human Sacrifice

This was practised especially among the tribes along the South-East Coast. Here scalps taken in battle **scalpings** were treated as sacrificial objects. Sacrifice was also thought to appease the spirits as well as to gain higher status in society. It was not unknown for men to sacrifice their own children at public ceremonies, but usually war captives were sacrificial victims. Sacrifices were made for other purposes such as to ensure good harvests, and bring about cures. People were not tortured in sacrifice but killed quickly.

Death

Some people were allowed to die in their house, after which the house might be torn down or burned, as this was believed to stop the ghost of the deceased from haunting it. In communal houses, a dying person was often moved to a special hut just before death.

Burial customs varied from group to group. Among the Inuit (Eskimos) the body of the deceased was usually left on top of the frozen ground as digging a grave was impossible. The North-West Coast people placed their dead in wooden boxes (coffins) which were put in canoes and sent out to sea. Caves and rock shelters were also used as graves, as well as hollow trees and logs. Cremation was practised among some tribes. In the northern Plains, burial on a scaffold or in a tree was practised.

Prayers

Prayers were offered in an attempt to obtain the help of spirits or supernatural powers. Often prayers accompanied sacrifices and people had to proceed through various rituals such as fasting and purification before prayers could be offered.

Calumet or Peace Pipe

This ceremonial pipe was smoked among men in most tribes. Agreements reached while the pipe was being smoked were regarded as binding and sacred.

Sweat Lodge rituals took place inside pole frameworks covered with buffalo hides. Tokens of prayers were made at sweat lodge rituals and were left fastened to trees. The red cloth represents an offering to the sun, the green to the earth, and the blue to the sky.

Initiation

Initiation was the most important ritual in any person's life. Young women and men went through an initiation to enable them to become full adult members. Initiation rituals took different forms in different societies but mostly they involved body scarification and dancing, singing and feasting.

Potlatch

This was a custom practised by many people, particularly those of the North-West Coast. Wealthy individuals would hold a feast to which a major rival would be invited. The main purpose of the potlatch was to give away prized possessions to a rival, who would then need to return the courtesy. Potlatches were held in association with important events such as marriages, births, deaths and initiations.

Sweating and Sweat Houses

Sweat bathing was widely practised, and sweat houses, which were similar in design, were built throughout the continent. The sweat house was large enough to accommodate several people at one time.

Near the floor a large hole was dug into which were placed pre-heated stones. These were then sprinkled with water to create steam. The people inside would expose themselves to this steam for about half an hour after which the bather would plunge into the cold water of a stream.

The sweat bath ritual was undertaken for three purposes:
Religious and Ceremonial It was used as a means of purifying the body as this was thought to appease the spirits.
Medical Sweat baths were often a part of cures, and the shaman often sang outside the sweat house while the patient was inside.
Social Among some groups going to the sweat house was a daily social custom.

Obeying the Law

In all Indian societies, the laws and rules which people lived by were taught by the family and by other adults, and were enforced by the leaders and the shamans. All groups had their leaders. The head of an Inuit (Eskimo) village was usually the most capable hunter and the shaman because the people believed his powers were also important.

Taboos

Taboos or prohibitions were placed on people, food, objects, places and behaviours for many different reasons. For example there were taboos observed by boys and girls undergoing initiation ceremonies, by women before the birth of a child, by relatives after a person's death, by hunters, and by shamans while effecting cures.

The breaking of any taboo, once it was declared, was punishable in all societies.

Truth, honesty and the safeguarding of life were the basis for Indian rules of living, and their unwritten laws revolved around this.

Some Indian Crimes and Punishments

In Inuit society, to eat both caribou and seal meat at the one meal, was considered greedy and an insult to the sensitive souls of both species. Punishment was decided by the local shaman, and failure to carry out this punishment meant being banished from the community.

Murder in some societies was punishable after trial, by execution. Murder in self-defence was regarded as just.

Among the Cheyenne of the Plains, only three crimes were recognised: homicide, disobeying the rules of the buffalo hunt and, in later times, repeated horse theft. Homicide was punishable by banishment for 5 to 7 years.

For disobeying the rules of the buffalo hunt, the punishment was a beating, often a severe one, and the destruction of the person's property. This was also the punishment given for horse theft.

The Iroquois, Huron and Algonquian of the Eastern Forests and their neighbours often settled disputes involving death with "blood money" that is, compensation paid to the family of the slain person in the form of **wampum**.

Inuit woodcarving of a shaman in the middle of a seance. The two animal-like creatures beside him are his helping spirits. The drum, which is also beside him, was used to conjure spirits. The shaman was usually the head of an Inuit community.

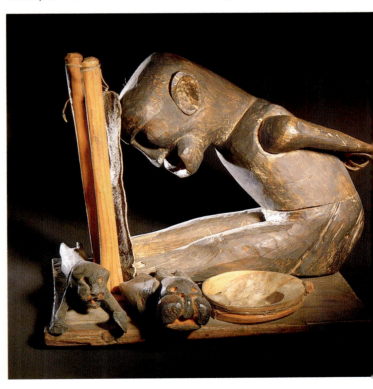

Writing it Down: Recording Things

It has been estimated that there were 3,200 different languages spoken by the first Americans prior to the arrival of the Europeans, but the Aztec, Maya and nearby Meso-American people were the only ones to possess a system of writing.

The way things were recorded in Indian societies without writing was to commit things to the collective memory of the people. Specialised knowledge such as religious laws, taboos, medical knowledge, histories, and knowledge about hunting and food gathering areas was vested in individuals who were carefully selected. They were also charged with the responsibility of teaching this knowledge to someone who would succeed them.

Pictographic and Ideographic Writing

Pictographs were a form of conveying ideas by means of pictures or marks They are closely related to sign language at which the first Americans were highly skilled.

Pictographs were recorded on a variety of objects (the favourite being people's bodies) including stone, bone, skins, gourds, shells, earth and hard wood. From this earliest form of picture writing the figure became more standardised until it became a symbol or **glyph**.

Rock carvings are common in most areas of North America, but are difficult to understand. They may have been boundary markers, records of important matters or magical symbols.

Sign Language

Sign language was often used with people who were unable to understand each other's languages. It was used mainly among the nomadic people such as the Indians of the Great Plains who moved around a defined area (in search of food) and frequently came upon other people.

Wampum

These were shell beads assembled in strings or woven into belts. Wampum belts had coloured beads arranged in such a way as to convey meanings and were primarily used as records of important agreements or treaties. The word is derived from *wampumpeag* which means "strings of white shell beads". Wampum was also used as money in some places during the 17th and 18th centuries, and by some western Indians until the middle of the 19th century.

Calendars

The first Americans relied on a seasonal calendar and became expert at reading the signs of nature such as the flights of particular birds, the changes in sea currents, cloud and wind patterns, and slight changes in vegetation. In the far north, years were counted as "so many snows" and in areas where snow was rare, reference was made to "the heat of the sun".

Most Eastern Forest tribes divided the year into five or six seasons. The most important time division was the moon, or month beginning with the new moon.

People generally calculated years by some remarkable event or phenomena which took place. Notched sticks were often kept as records of time, while others kept symbolic figures or pictographs.

Part of an Inuit ivory bow drill handle which contains incised sketches of hunting and travel scenes. Bone and ivory handles were popular places for people to record events and views of daily life.

Counting

Counting was based on a finger and hand count, that is to the number 5.

For example $6 = 5+1$; $7 = 5+2$, and so on.

On the Atlantic coast, all except the Inuit (Eskimos) used a decimal system based on this finger and hand count.

Legends and Literature

Without writing as we know it, the first Americans committed everything of importance to memory. To prompt their memory paintings, figures, carvings, sand paintings, and songs and stories of tribal heroes and spirits were made. Each group had its own literature and legends preserved in different ways. Legends were tied to religion and were used to explain the world to people in terms which made sense. Some anthropologists have attempted to collect various myths and legends of the first Americans and, in the second half of the 20th century, have made attempts to publish them.

Poetry

Most rituals were classed as poetry with thoughts being expressed in a dignified language. Some of these were chanted while others were sung. Those chanted often had drawn out sounds in order to make the sound recur in a particular kind of repeating pattern. These chants were often performed with other rituals such as the waving of feathered emblems, altar decorations or with special postures and marches.

Some Legends of the First Americans

Group	About the legend
The Haida of North-West Coast	There were several legends about the creator and trickster Raven who brought gifts to the people. Raven was supposed to have been reborn as a grandson to a fisherman who kept the moon inside ten boxes, one inside the other. His grandfather gave Raven the moon as a playtoy which he threw up to the sky where it remained.
Cree of the Sub-Arctic	The trickster (a spirit) was trying to trap beavers who kept flooding the land by using magic. The trickster, assisted by Wolf, devised other magic which made moss grow over the water, thereby creating the world.
Navaho of the South-West Desert	Glispa, a young girl, was abducted by a Snake man and taken to the underworld where the Snake People lived. She returned after two years and brought with her the secrets of healing which she taught to her brother, the shaman.
Abnaki [Wabanaki] of the North-East and Great Lakes	A man of the tribe once met a beautiful woman with long silken hair. She taught him first how to make fire and then how to grow maize or corn. To this day the corn still grows long silken hair to remind them of the corn maiden who shook her hair over the land to make the corn grow.
Sioux of the Great Plains	An old man named Waziya lived with his wife beneath the earth. Their daughter married the wind and bore four sons, the winds of the North, East, West and South. Together with the Sun and the Moon they controlled the universe. There are many legends about their adventures and powers.

Art and Architecture

Although there was a great variety in the art produced by the different North American Indian cultures, there existed basic concepts that underlied all Indian art. All art had to serve social purposes, in that it could be used in religious and other ceremonies. Art was also used to indicate status within a society, and was a means of communication.

Because many of the first American people were nomadic, their art objects had to perform a useful service. This reflected the essential character of the society. In groups where warfare was emphasised, the major art was in the form of weapons; in others with a religious emphasis, ceremonial art objects were designed to please the spirits. Many items served a dual function: for example, bowls used everyday were also used during ceremonies. However, not all art served religious or political purposes, and many items were intended to be humorous or personally pleasing.

Art objects were traditionally made from a variety of materials found in the natural environment, including shell, bone, feathers, animal skins, wood, stone, clay, and vegetable fibres. Those people who lived in areas where forests grew, used wood extensively and produced much wooden sculptures and carvings. Where there was plenty of clay, pottery was the main medium.

Materials were carved, engraved, modelled, baked, painted, woven, tied, twined and braided. The process by which an object was created was often as important as the object itself, and often involved complicated rituals.

Broadly, traditional styles of Indian art can be classified according to the main North American cultural areas.

Inuit mask from Alaska that represents a supernatural being. Many masks represented the spirits of animals or supernatural beings. When an actor put on such a mask during a ritual, he became imbued with the spirit of the mask.

Inuit (Eskimo) Art

This consisted of carving and engraving in wood, bone, horn and ivory. Most carving and engraving were done as decoration on everyday objects such as knife handles and dishes, and depicted everyday life. The largest objects made by the Inuit were carved masks (usually wood) which were worn during religious ceremonies in Greenland and Alaska.

The Indians of the Plains recorded their war and hunting exploits in pictographic drawings, as shown on this model tipi cover.

Basketry of the Californian People

Art scholars have proclaimed that no other people in the world have produced such a large variety of superb basketry as the Indians of California. Many of their artists were able to produce such tight weaves that they were used for watertight containers.

North-West Coast

Wood carvings and crests were the dominant art form in the North-West. Figures of animals, monsters and humans were carved into most objects including totem poles, masks, canoes and houses. These carvings represented supernatural ancestral beings. Motifs were also carved in stone, bone, ivory and painted on hide as well as woven into basket and blanket designs. This art work was always regarded as men's work although women often did the actual craftwork after the male artist had completed the design. Most art objects were used to identify rank, and were displayed as symbols of wealth.

Hide Art of the Plains

The most popular art material used by the Plains Indians was buffalo hide. Hides were used to make cloaks, shirts, moccasins, tipi covers and linings, and shields. Colours used in painting were brown, red, yellow, black, blue and green, all of which were obtained from vegetable matter. Men were the painters of naturalistic figures while women painted geometric designs. Women mainly decorated containers and tipis. Porcupine quill embroidery was also the work of women. The quills were softened in water, flattened and dyed, and then worked into a dressed hide.

The South-West

The peoples of the South-West mainly produced items of everyday use, including decorative basketry, pottery, woven cloth, ceremonial objects, and wall and sand paintings.

Coiled baskets were made at least 2,000 years ago. Pottery decorated with painted designs was made by villagers in southern Arizona, from A.D. 200 onwards, and soon became a popular artform throughout the region. Figurative designs were painted on some pottery pieces, but the most predominant decoration on pottery was black lines and other geometric patterns on a pale background.

Ceremonial objects included the stone and wood sculpture masks used by the Kachina dancers. Underground religious chambers known as **Kivas**, had impressive wall paintings. Sand paintings using sand dyed with natural pigments were made by the Pueblos for their Kivas.

The Navajo people further developed sand paintings. They also produced textiles, and beautiful silver and turquoise jewellery.

Navaho sand painting design, circa 1880. Sand paintings were done in a sacred manner according to ancient knowledge. This design shows two supernatural beings flanking the sacred maize plant, and surrounded by the spirit of the rainbow.

Going Places: Transportation, Exploration and Communication

The American Indians travelled everywhere on foot or by canoe. Loads were carried on a wheeless dog-drawn vehicle. In later times, the Europeans introduced horses, which replaced dogs in pulling these loads. Often women carried the loads to ensure that the men were ready to defend the group in the event of a surprise attack.

Dugout canoes, birch bark canoes, canoes made of tule and other grasses, and balsa craft were used to cross streams.

Inuit (Eskimos) used dog sleds for transport, with a team of six to eight dogs being able to haul a sled 32 to 48 kilometres (20 to 30 miles) a day. The Inuit also had hide covered boats called the **umiak**(women's boat) and the **kayak** (men's boat) which were propelled by paddles. The kayak was one of the most effective means of water travel in the world. Snow-shoes were also used to enable people to walk over snow and very soft ground. They were made with a wooden rim and crossbar of wood with rawhide thonging. Toboggans were another efficient means of transport.

Although kayak designs built by the Inuit varied in detail from one region to another, the basic plan of a slender, very fast hunting boat propelled by paddles never varied. The kayak below was built small enough for a boy of about 7 to 10 years to use so that he could acquire the skills necessary to be a successful hunter.

Detail of a robe made from rawhide with pictographs depicting a bison chase on horseback. This was the most popular method of hunting after the introduction of horses in the 17th century.

Trade

Most native American Indian societies traded with their neighbours. Sometimes certain tribes acted only as traders bringing together buyers and sellers, and at which time feasting, singing and dancing would also take place. Money as we know it did not exist, and trade took the form of **barter**. Chocolate beans (cacao) operated as a form of currency in some places as did wampum (shell beads) which were used in the eastern areas.

In later times, trade with Europeans brought permanent changes to Indian society generally. The Europeans sought furs, and the Indians soon learned to use horses and guns. The fur trade also encouraged the men of the tribes to leave their families and go on extended hunting expeditions. Animals became exploited for their hides and furs, and many tribes faced starvation as a result.

Communication

Because there were so many different languages, not all people who encountered each other, especially for trade reasons, were able to communicate. To solve this problem, sign language and signalling systems evolved.

Long distance signalling was used when the observer and the signaller could not see each other. The most common messages were those indicating the presence of game or danger.

Smoke signals were common. A fire was lit burning material which provided a dense smoke. Prescribed patterns were made by covering the smoke at intervals with bark or a blanket.

If the signaller could be seen, movement was used such as walking or riding in a circle or by holding a blanket or cloak in a special manner.

Drum signals were used for calling people together on special occasions.

Music, Dancing and Recreation

Songs were the main music of the North American Indians. Musical instruments were used mainly to provide rhythmic accompaniment.

Songs and Musical Instruments

Most music was a part of daily activities, rituals and ceremonies, and as men were the leaders in many of these activities they were also the leaders of singing, and makers and players of instruments.

Songs were of various kinds and included songs for games, gambling songs, teaching songs, lullabies (usually sung by women), love songs, boasting songs and joke songs. In some cultures, songs were regarded as personal property and could be inherited. Inuit (Eskimo) songs were usually slow tempo, accompanied by tambourine type drums. In Inuit culture "duelling" in the form of songs of ridicule was sometimes preferred to fighting.

In the southern areas harvest songs, ritual performance songs and songs for entertainment were the predominant form. Here there were song specialists, as rituals had to be performed without mistakes.

The most popular musical instruments of the North American Indians included various types of rattles, sticks, clappers, rods and drums. The Indians had a variety of drums including skin

Portrait mask from the North-West Coast. The symbols depict the character being portrayed during a dance performance. Portrait masks often had the same designs as those used in facial painting.

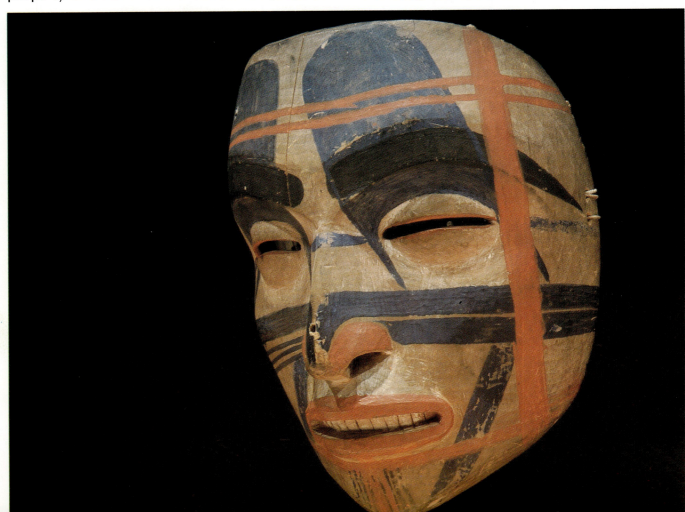

head drums, wooden kettle drums, **water drums**, bark cylinders and tambourines.

Dancing

In many places music was inseparable from dance. Both music and dancing were included in rituals such as war dances, curing ceremonies and initiation dances. Women had their own music, and it depended upon local customs and traditions as to whether men or women danced and if they danced separately or together.

Dancing costumes varied from group to group, and depended on the ritual. Women of the south-east (and shamans) wore turtle shells containing pebbles and bunches of deer hooves attached to their legs to produce a rattling sound when dancing. Inuit dancers shook mittens with attached puffin beaks and belts with animal teeth. Southern male dancers wore buckskin kilts to perform certain dances and Hopi dancers also wore deer hooves attached to a tortoise shell. Masks and headdresses were also used by many dancers and were designed to frighten the observers or to help the dancer to act out an existence other than their own. Costumes of feathers, body paint and drums were essential parts of dance display.

Pipe Smoking

The smoking of a pipe was a recreational act as well as a ceremonial act. The peace pipe was regarded as a communication between the spirits and people. Pipes were revered objects and were highly decorated. The decoration depended on the group and the occasion for which it was used.

Although Indian children of the Great Plains were very independent and made a wide variety of makeshift toys themselves, a large number of dolls were made by the older women for their grandchildren. This doll (shown right) is a Sioux human doll, made from rawhide and decorated with beadwork. It shows a woman's riding equipment and adult costume.

Games

Adult games included: archery (of various kinds); sliding javelins and darts along the ice or bare ground; shooting at a netter hoop and ring target; ball games of various kinds, and racing games.

Bows and arrows were used in most games and ceremonies, and were often a significant part of a game. Gaming objects and dress were often considered sacred. Cat's cradle, consisting of weaving patterns in a continuous string with the fingers, was another favourite pastime. The designs were difficult and intricate.

Juggling and stilt walking were also enjoyed as games. Dolls were common among many tribes, particularly the Inuit.

Wars and Battles

Before the Europeans introduced horses and guns to the American Indians, battles were fought between armies of hundreds of warriors on foot and armed with lances (spears), bows and arrows, and **tomahawks**, with hide armour and shields for protection. Poisoned arrows were used by some tribes and clubs were used in earlier times. Rituals preceeded battles and included special dances and body painting. Chiefs were important people who usually led battles.

The Indians recognised two kinds of warfare: defensive warfare for the protection of the people, and aggressive warfare which involved going off on expeditions to avenge or to obtain spoils of war.

After the introduction of horses and guns, warring parties became smaller and surprise raid attacks became common.

The first Americans fought bravely and consistently against the European invaders of their lands. However, the Europeans forced the Indians gradually westward and this often brought tribes into conflict with others upon whose land they were forced.

Feuds

Feuds and minor disputes between groups of native Indians had always occurred and each group had its own warriors for the defence of the group. Raids frequently occurred to obtain weapons, boats, clothing, hides, slaves and wives (and later horses) from other tribes, but this was not considered as large scale warfare.

However, not all native people were warlike. The people of the Californian region and the Pueblo people of the South-West Desert, were generally peaceful.

Warlike groups were largely confined to the Plains, the Prairies and to the groups of the east, with the Iroquois possibly having the largest fighting force. In these areas a young man needed to gain prestige as a warrior and often had a special name bestowed upon him to enhance his chances of marriage or holding a status position in the tribe. It was also considered necessary for war parties to return with a specified number of scalps or return in disgrace.

War parties used scouts who went in advance of the warriors and returned with information to help plan battle strategy. Communication between members of the war party was done by bird and animal cries and smoke signals. Camouflage was often used. Indians had the ability to move seiftly and efficiently.

Victory celebrations were held in which the whole tribe participated. The recounting of brave acts was common to ensure the society remembered, honoured and respected its warriors.

Forts were used for defensive warfare. The most common type was a hill fort where walls of earth or stone was heaped up around a peak or hilltop.

War drums were used to call people together to assemble an army. This would precede the sending of a declaration of war. The peace pipe or calumet had its place in war and peace ceremonies. If it was offered during battle and accepted, weapons on both sides were usually laid down. In some places, when war was contemplated, the shaft and feathers of the calumet were coloured red.

Opposite: detail of a painted buffalo hide, by the Great Plains Indians. The painting gives a good indication of war costume. The mounted figure has a long feather trailer which indicates his high status. He rides a painted pony whose tail has been tied up for war. The posture of the warriors in front of the rider is one of "no retreat".

Inventions and Special Skills

Domestication of Plants

Many plants domesticated and cultivated from their wild state by the Indians are, today, found in the diets of people around the world. Of particular importance are potatoes, sweet potatoes, maize, and manioc. Potatoes were originally grown by Indians of the south and were taken to Europe by the Spaniards in about 1570. They appeared in England in 1596, and in Ireland in 1606. Tobacco was an American non-edible plant which also found its way around the world.

Clothing Styles

The Western world has adopted many of the highly efficient clothing styles originally designed by the Indians. These included the parka, modelled on the garment of the Inuit (Eskimo); moccasins, which have been adopted as house slippers and outdoor shoes; ponchos, which are adaptations of rainwear and water-proof garments of the southern people.

Sign Language

A commonly understood system of silent communication within a group as well as between different groups was devised by the American Indians. This included sign language of various kinds from hand and arm signals, the arrangement of feathers or garments about a person or on weapons, to using blankets and cloaks held in various positions, or people standing, riding or walking in certain formations or directions and the signalling with smoke. It was not until the invention of the telegraph that Europeans could match the speed at which the first Americans communicated over long distances.

Porcupine Quill Work

This art form existed nowhere else in the world. Small quills of the American porcupine were flattened, dyed and applied to animal hides and textiles. Braids of quills were often wound around pipe stems. The art declined when Europeans introduced glass beads to the Indians who preferred the beads as the colours did not fade.

Words and Place Names

Many thousands of geographical place names commonly used in North America today are of Indian origin. Many native words have also been incorporated into everyday language such as tobacco, toboggan, moccasin, wampum, tipi and **wigwam**.

Hammock

This was an Indian invention, unknown to the Europeans. One of the first illustrations of a hammock appeared in a French book in 1625. It was later to become the standard sleeping place in European ships.

Efficient Transport

Although the first Americans did not use a wheeled vehicle they invented other highly efficient means of transport. Snowshoes, toboggans and kayaks have been adopted from the first Americans.

Why the Civilisation Declined

Before the arrival of the white settlers in the New World, it has been estimated that approximately one million Indians were scattered throughout the North American continent. By the 1850s, the Indians had been pushed into the western half of the continent, and by 1875, the Indians were limited to fourteen main reservations, which were areas of land specially set aside for the Indians.

Many people were completely dispossessed and moved at bayonet point. They were the victims of Europeans who had advanced technology in the form of guns and who considered themselves to be a superior people.

This idea that the white settlers were superior came about through their fear of an unknown culture. The Indians viewed the land they lived on differently to those who wanted to take it over. The Indians had a great respect for their land and did not believe in the concept of land ownership. To the Indians, the land was holy and belonged to everyone, as did the air, the skies and the waters. The Indians lived in harmony with nature and the land.

The white settlers' view of land ownership was contrary to the Indian beliefs. The white settlers believed that a person who owned land was a free person, and the more land a person owned, the richer that person became.

The white settlers' aim was to remove the Indians from the land they wanted to settle, and, as a result, they hunted and wiped out many tribes. In the wake of the first invading Europeans came the Christian missionaries who considered their religion to be superior and added their own brand of cultural destruction. They not only destroyed the native religions but persuaded the people to wear European clothes, learn European ways of reading, writing and living, and abandon the old ways.

As a result of the white conquest of North America, the first Americans lost their homes, tribal life, means of survival, cultural standards, religion and often their will to live. The European diseases, to which these people had no resistance, also took their toll. The Europeans criticised these people as weak and lazy, and overlooked their past pride, dignity, bravery, innovations and inventions.

Others understood what had happened to the people and reacted with anger at the Europeans' lack of compassion, concern and knowledge. In recent times there have been attempts to increase the pride and identity of the descendants of the first Americans. The first Americans were victims of European world colonisation.

Navaho Indian herding goats. Decendants of the first Americans still live in America today, though their population has been greatly reduced.

Glossary

Barter   To trade by exchange of commodities rather than money.

Birch Bark Canoe   A canoe made from the outer bark of the birch tree. The paper birch is so named because of its sheetlike layers of paper on its trunk. Bark peeled in spring when it was heaviest was shaped over a cedar frame and sewn with spruce roots. It was caulked with pine gum.

Breechcloth   A garment worn by men of the Great Plains consisting of a piece of buckskin passed between the legs and held in place at the back and front with a belt around the waist.

Candlefish   A seafish found on the north-west coast and used by the people for food and oil. The fish was so oily it could be dried and burnt like a candle.

Curare   A drug extracted from the bark and stem of certain vine plants, which relaxed the body. It is dark brown to black in colour and has a smell of tar. It acts on the body in a similar as an anaesthetic

Glyph   A character used in the writing devised by the first Middle Americans.

Gruel   Light thin cooked cereal made by boiling meal in water or milk.

Head Binding   A custom followed by many Indians where a baby's head was deformed by means of a cradle board bound to its head during the first year of life. The deformation persisted throughout life. A flattened head was a sign of beauty and of a freeperson in some societies.

Hominy   A food made by hulling, crushing and grinding maize and boiling it with water or milk.

Ideograph   A symbol representing the idea of something directly and not its written sound.

Igloo   A dome-shaped home made from blocks of ice and snow and used by the Inuit during winter.

Inuit (Eskimo)   A group of people native to North America who occupied nearly all the coasts and islands of Arctic America.

Jade   A semi-precious green stone used by people of Alaska and British Columbia. It was not quite as hard as quartz but was quite tough. It was used for implements, masks, statuettes and ornaments.

Kayak (kaiak)   An Eskimo boat used by men. It was made by stretching seal hide over a framework of whalebone or driftwood.

Landbridge   An area of land which connects major land masses.

Leaching   To cause water to percolate through something, to remove soluble constituents.

Manioc (cassava)   A plant cultivated throughout the tropical world. It has tuberous roots from which flour, breads, tapioca and an alcoholic drink can be made.

Moccasins   Soft leather shoes. There were two types of moccasins: those with a rawhide sole sewed to a leather upper (as worn by the eastern tribes), and those with sole and upper consisting of one piece of soft leather with a seam at the instep and heel (as worn by the Western and Plains people.) A boot or legging moccasin was worn in Alaska.

New World   This refers to the Western Hemisphere of the North and South American continents.

Old World   This refers to that part of the world known before the discovery of the Americas by Europeans and comprised Europe, Asia and Africa.

Parfletche   A skin container made from stiff dressed or rawhide from which all hair had been removed. It was folded together like an envelope to form a container in which belongings were carried.

Parka   An Eskimo upper outer garment made of two hides sewn together at the sides and with sleeves and a hood. Women's parkas were made large enough so a child could be carried next to the mother.

Pemmican A food preparation made by cutting meat into thin slices and drying it over a slow fire. To this was added melted fat and berries. This was compressed into skin bags in which, if kept dry, it could be preserved for 4 to 5 years but was usually eaten well before this time. Fish pemmican was made by people in the North-West. It was made of dried fish and sturgeon oil. The Inuit made pemmicans from chewed deer meat, deer suet and seal oil.

Pestle and Mortar Implements used for grinding grains for food.

Pictograph A form of thought-writing in which a person conveys ideas by means of picture signs or marks. They are closely connected to sign language.

Potlatch A winter ceremony. These were occasions which were marked by the giving away of one's wealth, often to the extent of extreme impoverishment. The return was increased esteem in the eyes of others. During the festival, houses and carved poles were raised, and the chief's children were initiated.

Rawhide The skins of large land and water animals were made into rawhide. In preparing rawhide the skin was fleshed, dehaired and stretched until it dried. Whole buffalo or cow skins were used to make boats. Deerskins, and seal and sea-lion skins were joined by sewing, and used to make canoes, kayaks and umiaks. Pieces of rawhide were made into parfletche, arrow cases, cases and pouches. Plains tribes used circular pieces of thick rawhide for pemmican or fruit mortars.

Scalping Name given to the Indian practice of removing a portion of haired skin from an enemy's head for trophy purposes. It was not exclusively an Indian practice. It was known to the ancient Greeks. Some scholars think that this practice might have been taught to the Indians by the Europeans.

Shaman This was a person who mediated between people and the spirits or supernatural. Their authority depended on their ability, and many became adept at predicting events from nature. They performed religious and healing functions and often held positions of political importance in a group or tribe.

Tipi The conical dwelling of the Plains people and those of the North-West, made from hides. It consisted of a circular frame-work of poles brought together and tied near the top and covered with dressed buffalo skins sewn to form a single piece. It was kept in place by wooden pins and tent pegs. Smoke escaped through the hole at the top.

Tomahawk A weapon commonly used by the Algonquian tribes of the east. It was used as a weapon of war as well as in ceremonies. It is thought to have evolved from the club. Some were finely engraved and painted, and decorated with feathers.

Totem An object of nature, usually an animal, adopted as a token emblem of a family or tribe.

Totem Poles Carved cedar poles erected by the people of the north Pacific coast and Alaska. There were inside and outside house poles and memorial columns. Carvings on grave posts were usually crests owned by the family of the deceased. Those on house posts could be crests or illustrations of stories, figures of the owner of the house or someone the owner wanted to ridicule. Those of the houses of the shamans were adorned with the shaman's spirit teachers.

Umiak A boat used by Eskimo women. It was made by stretching seal hide over a framework of whalebone or driftwood.

Water Drum An instrument made by stretching hide on a small wooden keg partly filled with water. It was used by the Iroquois and by shamans of the mid-west.

Wigwam Name for an Algonquian dwelling which was a conical structure made of saplings, bark and rushes.

The First Americans: Some Famous People and Places

Pocahontas

Pocahontas is probably the best known of the later American Indians. Her real name was Matoaka (Matowaka) which was derived from the Alonquian Metawake, to amuse oneself by playing, or playful. Her father used the word Pokahantes when speaking of her, which finally led to her being given the name Pocahontas.

She was said to have saved the prisoner Captain John Smith from the Powhatan's people. When Captain Smith departed for England in 1609, Pocahontas was kidnapped, taken on board the ship of Captain Argall in the Potomac and taken to Jamestown. Here in the place of the Powhatan chief, she was held for ransom.

While in the company of the English, she met John Rolfe whom she married in 1613 and this kept the peace between the colonists and the Powhatan.

In 1616 Pocahontas, accompanied by her husband, her brother-in-law Uttamatomac, Sir Thomas Dale and others, became the first woman of her race to visit England. She became ill at the beginning of her return voyage to her homeland and was taken ashore where she died at Gravesend. She was twenty-one at the time and her story made her a heroine in England.

William Ordway Partirdge's monument to Pocahontas stands in Jamestown, and a bronze replica was donated to St. George's Church, Gravesend, which was unveiled in 1958.

Geronimo

Geronimo is Spanish in origin, being applied to Jerome or Jeronimo as a nick name. Geronimo's real name was Goyathlay ("one who yawns"). Geronimo was a medicine man and prophet of the Chiricahua Apaches who resisted the white invaders and authorities. His grandfather had assumed to be a chief but his father was not a chief. His mother's name was Juana. In 1858, his mother, wife and children were killed by Mexicans.

When the Chiricahua were removed from their land by the United States Government in 1874, they were also required to accept Christianity. Geronimo and other younger important tribal members fled to Mexico. He returned and cultivated tribal lands for a time until the government refused to help the Chiricahua with irrigation schemes.

In 1882 Geronimo led one of the bands who surrounded the forces of General George J. Crook. He also led other bands during 1884–85 in an attempt to resist further colonisation of Indian lands. Crook sent out more forces who were instructed to capture or destroy Geronimo and his followers. Geronimo and 340 others were captured in 1886 and deported as prisoners of war to Florida, then Alabama and finally Oklahoma. Geronimo was promised he and his followers could eventually return to Arizona, but this promise was not kept. Instead these people were put to hard labour, far from their families.

Geronimo dictated his autobiography to S.S. Barrett, and was published. He has been recognised by General Crook and others as being one of the greatest of his people.

Tenskwatawa and Tecumseh

Tenskwatawa (also called Elskwatawa) was a famous Shawnee prophet and twin brother of Tecumseh who became a Shawnee chief. Tenskwatawa, when 30 years of age, claimed he had powers of prophecy learned from the spirit world and he gathered a great deal of support to oppose the intrusion of white civilisation on the lands and customs of his people. He abandoned his original name of Lalawethika and adopted Tenskwatawa. He was confirmed by his people as a great prophet when he successfully predicted an eclipse of the sun in 1806.

The followers of Tenskwatawa and Tecumseh, who was also an ardent opponent of white intrusion into his people's territory, joined the British forces in the war of 1812, after which Tenskwatawa was granted a pension from the British government. Tenskwatawa died in 1837 but his grave is unmarked and unknown. Tecumseh fell in battle on October 5th 1813.

Scajawea

Scajawea, also called Bird Woman was born about 1786 near present day Idaho. She was a Shoshone Indian woman who, while carrying her infant son on her back, accompanied the Lewis and Clark Expedition in 1804–06.

She had been captured by an enemy tribe when she was only 12 years old and sold into slavery. She was eventually sold again to a fur trader, a Canadian name Toussaint Charbonneau. Meriwether Lewis and William Clark encountered Toussaint Charbonneau who was hired as an interpreter, and Scajawea and their infant son also joined the expedition.

The group in turn encountered a band of Shoshone led by Scajawea's brother, Cameahwait. This ensured the expedition's safety as did the knowledge that an Indian mother and child were accompanying the expedition through Indian territory.

There have been more memorials raised to honour her than to any other north American woman.

Pontiac

Pontiac was an Ottawa chief, born about 1720 who became a great leader of his people. He organised combined resistance to the invasion of his people's lands in the Great Lakes area. He devised general uprisings and the destruction of British forts and settlements. (He was for a short time on friendly terms with the British but would not acknowledge King George as a superior, only as an "uncle".)

By 1764, Pontiac, although the Indian forces has been successful, realised that the British would eventually win because of their greater numbers and advantage in tactics. He therefore concluded a peace treaty in 1766.

He was murdered in 1769 by a member of the Peoria Indians.

Pontiac is regarded as a leader of equal calibre to Tecumseh.

Sequoia

Sequoia was a Cherokee, born in 1760, the son of a white father and a Cherokee mother. He grew up in a tribe and became a hunter and fur trader, as well as a skilled craftsman in silverwork, and an inventor. A hunting accident made him a cripple and he turned his inventive mind to other things.

He began to realise the importance of reading and writing and, by 1809, he had begun to invent a system of writing suitable for the Cherokee language. His idea was accepted in 1821 and soon many thousands of his people were able to read and write in their language. In 1822–23 this was extended to the western division of the Cherokee, among whom Sequoia decided to live. By 1824 works were being translated into the Cherokee language and by 1828 a newspaper, the *Cherokee Phoenix* was established.

He died in Mexico in 1843.

Index

Acknowledgements

The author and publishers are grateful to the following for permission to reproduce copyright photographs and prints:

Australasian Nature Transparencies: (Jonathan Chester) p.9, (Bill Bachman) p.11, (Peter McDonald) p.12, (N.H.P.A.) pp.13, 14, (Silvestris) p.41; Coo-ee Historical Picture Library p.17; Werner Forman Archive: cover, pp.10, 15, 16, 18, 19, 21, 22, 25, 26, 27, 28, 29, 31, 32, 33, 34, 35, 36, 37, 39.

While every care has been taken to trace and acknowledge copyright, the publishers tender their apologies for any accidental infringement where copyright has proved untraceable. They would be pleased to come to a suitable arrangement with the rightful owner in each case.

Cover design, maps and art: Stephen Pascoe

First published 1989 by
THE MACMILLAN COMPANY OF AUSTRALIA PTY LTD
107 Moray Street, South Melbourne 3205
6 Clarke Street, Crows Nest 2065

Associated companies and representatives throughout the world.

National Library of Australia
cataloguing in publication data

Odijk, Pamela, 1942–
The first Americans.

Includes index.
ISBN 0 333 47780 4.

1. Indians of North America — Juvenile literature. I. Title. (Series: Odijk, Pamela, 1942–   . Ancient world).

970'.004'97

Set in Optima by Setrite Typesetters, Hong Kong
Printed in Hong Kong

Oceania | Europe | Africa

c50 000 B.C. Aborigines inhabit continent

40 000 Evolution of man

Oceania			Europe					Africa	
Australian Aborigines	Maori	Melanesians	Greeks	Romans	Angles, Saxons & Jutes	Britons	Vikings	Egyptians	First Africans

Time scale (B.C.): 8000, 7500, 7000, 6500, 6000, 5500, 5000, 4500, 4000, 3500, 3000, 2500, 2000, 1500, 1000, 500 — B.C./A.D. 0 — (A.D.) 500, 1000, 1500, 2000

Australian Aborigines
- 8000 — Torres and Bass Straits under water
- 7000 — Lake Nitchie settled
- 5000 — South Australian settlements
- 3500 — Ord Valley settlement
- 1500 (A.D.) — Dutch explorers sight Aborigines
- First White settlers

Maori
- Legend: Kupe found New Zealand and told people how to reach there
- Maori arrive
- Great Britain annexed New Zealand

Melanesians
- Europeans dominate
- Cook's voyages
- Christianity is introduced

Greeks
- 7000 — Neolithic Age / Settled agriculture
- 3000 — Bronze Age / Crete — palaces
- Mainland building
- 1000 — Dark Age
- Colonisation
- City-states established
- Classical Age
- Wars — lands extended
- Hellenistic Age
- Empire divided, lands lost.
- Culture enters new phase

Romans
- Rome found
- Republic established
- Rome expands through Italy and foreign lands
- Empire begins: Augustus — emperor
- End of Western Roman Empire

Angles, Saxons & Jutes
- Hengist and Horsa arrived in Kent
- England: 12 kingdoms
- Athelstan rules all England
- Norman Conquest

Britons
- 4000 — Hunting and gathering
- 2000 — Megalithic monuments raised
- 1000 — Farms and buildings established
- Ogham alphabet in use
- Roman invasion
- Britain becomes two provinces
- Saxons settle

Vikings
- 8000 — The Baltic — freshwater lake
- 3000 — The first farmers
- 1500 — Bronze Age
- Celtic Iron Age
- Roman Iron Age
- Vendel period
- Army invade England
- Christianity adopted
- Viking laws recorded

Egyptians
- 5000 — Egypt-early farms
- 3500 — Predynastic
- 2500 — Old Kingdom / Giza pyramids
- 2000 — Middle Kingdom
- 1500 — New Kingdom
- 1000 — New Kingdom declines
- Persian conquest
- Greek conquest
- Roman rule

First Africans
- Farm settlements
- 5000 — Increased trade across Sahara
- 2000 — Sahara becomes desert
- 1000 — Kushites
- Nok
- Greek influence
- Kushites' power ends
- Arabs settle coast
- Christian European ship trade
- Europeans divide Africa